Original title:
Petal Power Poems

Copyright © 2025 Creative Arts Management OÜ
All rights reserved.

Author: Gideon Shaw
ISBN HARDBACK: 978-1-80566-644-8
ISBN PAPERBACK: 978-1-80566-929-6

Nature's Gentle Whispers

In the woods where squirrels dance,
A frog jumps in, loses its chance.
The flowers giggle, colors bright,
Waving hello in pure delight.

The bees do cha-cha on the blooms,
While ants march past in tiny plumes.
A gust of wind, a leaf takes flight,
Just like my hat, oh what a sight!

Through the Garden's Lens

Through the lens of a bumblebee,
I see a world so grand and free.
Roses blush and daisies tease,
Whispering secrets with the breeze.

The carrots wear their leafy caps,
While lettuce joins in funny japs.
I spy a worm with jokes to share,
Making everyone laugh in despair.

Aroma of Strength

Oh, the smell of basil's might,
Makes spaghetti dance with delight.
Thyme sings songs of strength and cheer,
As garlic whispers, 'Come over here!'

Chili peppers bring the heat,
While onions play a tearful beat.
Together they form a merry team,
Cooking up laughter, a flavorful dream.

Beauty in the Breeze

The dandelions, bold and proud,
Blow wishes to the gathering crowd.
Butterflies tease with winks so sly,
While grasshoppers leap and flap their tie.

A sunbeam tickles a cat's ear,
As it stretches out with zero fear.
Nature's giggles dance in the air,
Making us laugh without a care.

Starlit Petals

Under the moon, flowers giggle,
Chasing the stars, they dance and wiggle.
Bees buzzing tunes in a comical way,
While daisies wear slippers and sway all day.

Tulips in tuxes, the fashionista crew,
Throwing a ball with a confetti dew.
Roses gossip, all fragrant and bright,
Who knew flowers could party all night?

The Pulse of Petals

Petals tap dance on breezy floors,
With beats that make ants join in the roars.
Sunflowers strut in a rhythm divine,
While lilacs groove with a twist of their spine.

Dandelions blow, sending wishes to flight,
Confetti of fluff, oh what a sight!
Laughter erupts from the buds all around,
In this florally funny, petal-shaped sound.

The Poise of the Pansy

Pansy with poise, stands straight and proud,
Telling the tulips, "Don't you be loud!"
With a wink and a nod, she flips her petal,
In this garden, she's quite the rebel.

Petunias gossip, their petals in a swirl,
While violets laugh, giving twirls and a whirl.
With humor so bright, they all start to beam,
Is it flowers or comedians? Who would deem!

Mosaic of Nature

In a riot of colors, a scene of delight,
Each flower a canvas, bursting with light.
Marigolds chuckle, lilacs take flight,
With zinnias snickering, what a sweet sight!

The daisies play hide and seek with the sun,
While the hydrangeas giggle, having their fun.
Nature's a jester in bloom and in cheer,
Who knew that laughter could grow in the year?

Silent Unfurling

In the garden, I tiptoe low,
Daisies whisper, 'Hey there, slow.'
Roses turn red, jealous of my dance,
They wave their thorns, not giving a chance.

Butterflies giggle, making a fuss,
While the sun laughs, no need to rush.
I twirl and spin, causing a stir,
Plants look on, 'Who's that blur?'

Floral Dreams

In my dreams, flowers wear hats,
Sunflowers chat with sneaky cats.
Violets crack jokes, tulips roll eyes,
While daisies hum tunes, oh what a surprise!

I asked a rose for makeup advice,
It said, 'Sweetie, just add some spice!'
Lily laughed, 'Best not to fret,
In this bloom game, I bet you're a pet!'

Tides of the Tulips

Tulips surfing on a breeze,
Catching laughs with such great ease.
A daffodil belly flops, whoops!
While hydrangeas cheer from their flower loops.

Petals fit for a party, all aglow,
Throwing petals like confetti, just watch the show!
Pansies juggle, what a sight to behold,
In this garden antics, we're never too old.

Courage in Lavender

Lavender stands tall, full of sass,
Says, 'I'm the coolest flower in the grass!'
With a wink and a nod, it struts with pride,
While bees giggle, buzzing alongside.

'Bring on the rain, and I'll still glow bright,
Gonna dance in the storms, just wait for the night!'
Even wilted petals crack a grin,
In this floral world, let the fun begin!

Petals in the Wind

A flower sneezes, petals fly,
They dance around, oh my, oh my!
Bees start buzzing, think they're cool,
But end up stuck—what a silly fool!

Daisies giggle, tulips tease,
The wind just laughs, with gentle breeze.
Petals swirl like confetti bright,
Nature's party, what a sight!

Love Letters from the Garden

Roses write, in fragrant ink,
In garden beds, they laugh and wink.
"Dear Sunflower, you're such a star,
But don't forget, I'm not too far!"

The daisies sigh, "We're so misunderstood,
But our jokes? They're really quite good!"
With bees as postmen, fluttering by,
They deliver love notes, oh my, oh my!

Whispering Violet Dreams

Violets whisper, secrets shared,
"I've got a crush, but I'm quite scared!"
A dandelion blows, and off it goes,
Spreading wishes, and tickling toes.

Butterflies giggle, they think it's sweet,
As flowers sway to a quirky beat.
Though petals dream of distant skies,
They just can't help but laugh and rise!

The Journey of a Rose

A little rose, dressed up so fine,
Sets out exploring, feeling divine.
"I'll see the world, I'll make it bright,"
With thorns for protection—what a sight!

She meets a daisy, laughs a lot,
"Your petals are cute, but I'm still hot!"
They travel together, spreading cheer,
In a garden of giggles, nothing to fear!

Garden of Serenity

In the garden, weeds are proud,
They dance in breezes, bold and loud.
Sunflowers wear their sunny smiles,
While carrots hide in leafy piles.

Rabbits gossip, playful and spry,
Chasing each other as clouds drift by.
The daisies chuckle, petals sway,
As ants parade their own ballet.

The tomatoes blush with every sun,
While peppers joke, 'We're the funny ones!'
The onions cry, but not from shame,
In this garden of laughter, all play the game.

Amidst the joy, each bloom's a friend,
Nature laughs, and the fun won't end.
A symphony of colors bright,
In this happy place, all feels right.

Colors of the Soul

The tulips boast their hues so bright,
Their rivalry brings flowers to fight.
'I'm the red, the best!' one claims,
While violets giggle and throw their names.

The roses flirt with bees and breeze,
While daffodils dance with graceful ease.
'We're the stars of spring,' they tease,
As butterflies flutter, happy to please.

Marigolds cheer with yellow glee,
'Summer's here, come dance with me!'
The lilacs pout, 'What about us?'
But they join in the fun, not making a fuss.

With laughter colored in every bloom,
Each shade brings joy, dispelling gloom.
In this vibrant patch, oh so merry,
The colors of joy are bright and cheery.

Capturing Fleeting Beauty

Look at the blossom, time's cruel jest,
It blooms a moment, then takes a rest.
'Hold onto me!' the petals shout,
As the wind comes knowing what it's about.

A butterfly lands, but just for a snack,
With a wink and a nod, it's gone in a whack.
'You can't catch beauty,' the flowers sigh,
But they still flaunt their charm, oh my!

The breeze giggles, carrying scents,
As the petals drop, but there's no pretense.
'Enjoy the now!' they whisper with glee,
For fleeting moments are wild and free.

So come and laugh where the blossoms play,
Let your heart dance, come what may.
For though they fade, a new bloom shall rise,
In this merry garden, joy never dies.

The Embrace of the Lilies

The lilies lounge upon the pond,
With petals soft and whispers fond.
They float like dreams, in a lazy swirl,
While frogs and fish join in the whirl.

'How grand we are!' the lilies sing,
As dragonflies make their dance a fling.
'We're the queens of this watery ball,
Come join our fun; you're welcome, all!'

The frogs croak loudly, adding their flair,
With a splash and a leap, they float without care.
While the sun winks down, casting its rays,
The lilies laugh in the warm sun's blaze.

In this lovely embrace, so bright and free,
Nature chuckles with joy, just let it be.
So find your fun in blossoms and streams,
For life in the garden is made of dreams.

Petal Kisses

In the garden, bees do dance,
While flowers wear their best romance.
A tulip winks with a rosy grin,
She whispers jokes about the wind.

With soft breezes playing tricks,
The daisies tell their cheeky picks.
A daffodil, with sass, does sway,
And shares a laugh on sunny day.

The Softest Caress

A lily winks, her fragrance bold,
Yet claims she's shy, or so I'm told.
The roses giggle, petals bright,
They tease the bees who zoom in flight.

Each bloom a cheeky little sprite,
They plot and scheme from morn till night.
With gentle rustles, they conspire,
To tickle noses, lift spirits higher.

When Flowers Speak

If flowers had the gift of speech,
They'd share the secrets that they teach.
A peony would launch a jest,
While orchids boast of their soft dress.

The sunflowers' tall tales stand strong,
Of cheeky chats they have all day long.
In their whispers, laughter blooms,
As petals giggle through their rooms.

Colors of Reflection

In hues so bright, they love to play,
Each color stands in a funny way.
The violets snicker, the reds do cheer,
While greens grow jealous when blue buds near.

With laughter splashed from bloom to bloom,
They pull the sun into their room.
In a rainbow's arc, they skip and sway,
Colorful banter lights the day.

The Song of the Daisies

Daisies dance in the breeze,
Wiggling like they have knees.
They gossip about the sun,
While trying not to run.

With their faces all so bright,
Chasing clouds in sheer delight.
They laugh when raindrops fall,
Saying, "Water's not so tall!"

Each petal shines a bit,
Silly thoughts that they transmit.
When a bee comes buzzing near,
They giggle, then disappear.

Underneath the sky so wide,
With friends none can divide.
These flowers know the score,
Laughing always, wanting more.

Wishing on a Blossom

A blossom whispers a wish,
As bees join for a sweet dish.
"Make me a pie!" it asks the breeze,
"And sprinkle it with tiny peas!"

When the wind starts to play,
It makes the petals sway.
"Catch a cloud and take a ride!"
The florets squeal with pride.

In a garden full of dreams,
Everything is not what it seems.
They'd rather dance in a sprout,
Than figure what life's about.

Each bloom wishes on a star,
Thinking big, not too far.
With petals glowing in the night,
They giggle at their silly plight.

In the Shade of Blossoms

Underneath the branches lush,
Sitting still in a gentle hush.
Blossoms share their fun-filled tales,
As butterflies dance and flail.

A squirrel jumps with boundless glee,
Trying hard to climb a tree.
The flowers chuckle with delight,
"You look funny in mid-flight!"

They make games of hide and seek,
Losing petals, oh so cheeky.
When a breeze swoops down to play,
They sway and smile the day away.

In the shade where laughter grows,
Even the sun starts to doze.
It's a party, wild and free,
With blossoms as the VIP.

The Art of Shedding

Leaves drop down with such a flair,
"Look at me! I do not care!"
One by one, the petals fall,
Creating quite the colorful sprawl.

Flowers toss their dying cheer,
Laughing loud that autumn's near.
"We drop down just to make space,
For new blooms to join the race!"

The ground becomes a quilt of hues,
With colors bright like summer's blues.
They plot and plan their bold escape,
In a colorful, leaf-strewn drape.

It's an art, this shedding bliss,
Each flower giving goodbye with a kiss.
Amid the chaos and the cheer,
They whisper, "Next spring, we'll reappear!"

Whispers of the Blossoms

In the garden, flowers sigh,
Tickling bees as they float by.
Dandelions wear crowns of fluff,
Laughing at the clouds, so tough.

Tulips in a playful row,
Wink at squirrels, stealing the show.
Roses strut in colors so bright,
While violets giggle, quite a sight.

Petunias gather, sharing a joke,
Even the weeds start to poke.
Carnations dance with a cheerful grin,
Letting the sunshine draw them in.

Laughter blossoms, joy takes flight,
In this garden, pure delight.
Nature's jesters, bright and true,
Join the fun, there's space for you!

Dance of the Delicate

Butterflies spin, oh what a sight,
Waltzing along in the warm sunlight.
Lilies sway in their pastel hues,
Singing sweet songs, the giggling muse.

Jasmine whispers to the breeze,
While daisies sway with graceful ease.
Chasing shadows as they prance,
In this flowery, joyful dance.

Sunflowers turn, with heads held high,
Doing their best to reach the sky.
They cheer on the bees as they flip and twirl,
In this garden ballet, oh what a whirl!

Every bloom has a story to tell,
Through laughter and fragrance, we find our spell.
Come join the fun in nature's wide space,
Where humor and beauty interlace.

Garden Reverie

In the quiet of the garden nook,
Where seedlings chat and seeds get shook.
Zinnias gossip, nibbling on treats,
While sunlit daisies share their sweets.

Cucumbers chuckle in their green attire,
As marigolds sit by the campfire.
A rhubarb's grin, so red and bold,
Whispers secrets of treasures untold.

Tomatoes wear hats from gardening lore,
Flaunting their ripeness, what a score!
With every breeze, they sprinkle joy,
A playful glimpse of nature's toy.

So gather 'round, let laughter bloom,
In this colorful, fragrant room.
The magic's here, just take a look,
Open your heart, let joy overcook!

Fragrant Echoes

Lavender giggles in the warm air,
As bumblebees hum without a care.
Peonies blush, they've caught the sun,
Painting smiles, oh what fun!

Marshmallows growing on cotton grass,
Lollypops sprouting in leafy mass.
Lilies play hide and seek with the breeze,
Chasing shadows, bending their knees.

Sunset blooms in oranges and pinks,
Even the soil wears joyful winks.
Chrysanthemums throw a party at night,
Under the stars, oh what a sight!

The scents and giggles swirl all around,
In this fragrant world where fun is found.
Join the laughter, let your heart sway,
In this garden, we'll dance and play!

A Tapestry of Colors

In the garden, colors clash,
The roses wink, the daisies flash.
Tulips wearing funky hats,
Mimicking the cats and bats.

Bees are buzzing, can't you see?
Dancing 'round like it's a spree.
Colors swirling, bees on break,
Flower jokes, oh what a quake!

Laughter blooms in shades so bright,
Sunflowers giggle in delight.
Each petal whispers, 'Life's a jest!'
In this garden, we're the best!

So let's all join the floral fun,
Where laughter reigns, and worries shun.
Dress in color, don your cheer,
In this realm, there's nothing drear!

Gentle Touch of Nature

A butterfly lands on my nose,
Tickling me like a silly pose.
Grass blades giggle, tug at your shoe,
Nature's tickles, all anew!

The wind whispers, 'What a day!'
As squirrels join in a wild ballet.
A bloom sneezes, pollen flies,
Coughing flowers, oh what a surprise!

Every leaf plays peek-a-boo,
Nature's creams, a pastel hue.
With petals soft as jokes well told,
Nature's antics never get old!

So let's skip, roll, and twirl around,
With every laugh a joy unbound.
Nature's giggles fill the air,
Join in the fun, if you dare!

Heartstrings of the Orchid

An orchid dressed in velvet pink,
Winks at me with a cheeky blink.
Hearts a-flutter, in shock, oh dear!
Who knew they carried such good cheer?

This flower seems to tell a tale,
Of blossoms merry, without fail.
Whispers sweet of love's embrace,
In floral realms, it's quite the place!

The petals sway, a dance of charm,
Leaving all my worries, balm.
With every bloom, a silly grin,
Sparks of joy from deep within!

So if you find an orchid fine,
Join their laughter, share a line.
For who knew love could be so fun?
In every petal, life's a pun!

Echoes of Blooming Love

In a garden where romances play,
Lovebirds chirp in a silly way.
Roses sing a sweet refrain,
While tulips poke fun, not in vain.

A daisy's wink, a dandy chance,
To join the flowers in a dance.
Love notes flutter from bee's wings,
An orchestra of joyful things!

Lilies roll their eyes in jest,
As nature points out who's the best.
In rhymes and blooms, sweet tales untold,
Nature's humor, too bold to hold!

So take a stroll through bloom and cheer,
Where laughter spills and love is near.
Join the echoes, let them soar,
In this garden, we want more!

A Canvas of Color

With hues of red and shades of blue,
The flowers dance, they know what to do.
They whisper secrets, they giggle and sway,
Painting the garden in a bright, wild way.

In polka dots and stripes, they flaunt their flair,
Bumblebees buzz, with pollen to share.
Daisies don hats, with a daffodil tie,
Each bloom has a story, oh my, oh my!

Tulips make jokes, while roses just pout,
Sunflowers grin, trying not to shout.
Their laughter spreads, tickling the breeze,
In this blooming party, who needs to tease?

So when you're feeling a bit dull or gray,
Remember the flowers and their quirky display.
In the joyous riot, take a light-hearted peek,
For nature's a painter, with laughter to speak.

The Splendor of Simplicity

A single bloom stands tall and proud,
With petals so simple, it draws a crowd.
No frills, no fuss, just a bright sunny face,
In the field of wildflowers, it's a charming embrace.

A daisy grins wide, with a wink and a nod,
Telling the weeds, 'Don't you dare applaud!'
While clovers play tricks, hiding under the sun,
A simple bouquet can still be so fun!

Oh, lilacs giggle, they grow in straight lines,
They share all their stories, like old friends with wines.
These simple delights bring joy to our hearts,
In the garden's laughter, each day a new start.

So cherish the moments when life seems too grand,
And find joy in small things, like grains of sand.
For sometimes the simplest, can brighten our way,
Like a goofy flower that's ready to play!

The Veil of Blossoms

Underneath the canopy, blossoms in disguise,
They flutter and flap, like jesters in the skies.
A curtain of colors, they twirl in delight,
Making the garden feel perfectly bright.

With lilacs gossiping, and tulips in jest,
Each flower agrees that they're truly the best.
A rose in a tutu, so fancy and bold,
While violets whisper secrets only they hold.

Jasmine scents the air, with a giggle or two,
While daisies debate who has the best view.
They tease the tall sunflowers, who think they're the kings,
In this whimsical garden, oh, the joy that it brings!

So lift the veil gently, and step into play,
Join in the laughter on this bright, sunny day.
For in the realm of blossoms, there's giggles galore,
A hilarious haven, forever in bloom more!

Petal Wishes

In the garden, dreams do sprout,
Wishes flying all about.
A daisy's dance, a tulip's twirl,
Can make a grumpy gnome unfurl.

Bees are buzzing, oh so loud,
While flowers mingle with the crowd.
A daffodil trips in delight,
Causing giggles, such a sight!

When roses wear their Sunday best,
They try to impress all the rest.
But a clumsy bloom just stumbles,
In the breeze, it hilariously tumbles.

Sunflowers laughing, heads held high,
Think they're wiser, oh my, oh my!
While lilacs gossip, full of sass,
In floral banter, all class, no class.

With each breeze, there's a new joke,
Here's a chuckle from that oak.
In this garden, joy's the rule,
Nature's nonsense is the fuel.

The Exquisite Fade

Once a bloom with colors bright,
Flaunting glory, pure delight.
But time, that rascal, came to tease,
And left behind a garden sneeze.

With petals falling, what a fuss,
A floppy flower raised a cuss!
'I'm still fabulous, can't you see?'
But all that's left is a wilted spree.

Roses blush, but not for pride,
As they're wilting side by side.
Tiny daisies laugh and giggle,
While over here, old tulips wiggle.

Their vintage charm is quite renowned,
As faded magic spins around.
And though they lack their youthful gleam,
They still remind us—life's a dream!

With every wrinkle, there's a tale,
In the garden, quirks prevail.
So raise a glass to bloom and fade,
In this wild floral masquerade.

Where Beauty Meets Time

In the garden where time does prance,
Beauty twirls in a silly dance.
Sunshine giggles as it plays,
With wildflowers in a daze.

Dandelions boast, 'We're tough and fine!'
While daisies check their flowery line.
'You may be pretty, oh so sweet,
But I can keep my roots in the heat!'

Tangled vines, a jumbled mess,
Are trying hard to look their best.
But when they do, they trip and fall,
Spreading laughter, joy to all.

Time whispers secrets to each bud,
'Embrace your chaos, let life be fun!'
Yet here's the giggle—time does tease,
Beauty's fleeting, like a breeze.

In this realm of blooms and laughs,
A crocus plots its funny gaffes.
For in the end, the times we share,
Are filled with smiles, sweet fragrance in air.

Blossoms of Courage

In the face of wind, flowers sway,
Making jokes about 'this and that' play.
With petals fluffed, they stand so bold,
In the garden, stories unfold.

A brave little rose shouts, 'I'm tough!'
While butterflies scoff, 'Not enough!'
But truth be told through petals bright,
Courage blooms both day and night.

Daisies cheer with a clumsy stance,
As they waltz in a flowered dance.
'We may be small, but we don't care,
We'll face the storm with flair to spare!'

Lilacs whisper, 'Let's be grand!'
As they reach out a flowering hand.
Each blossom brimming with delight,
Fighting fears, taking flight.

The garden's pulse, a lively sound,
Where strength in bloom can still be found.
With every laugh, each playful stance,
Courage blooms—give joy a chance!

Secrets in the Soil

Worms can dance, don't you know?
They wriggle and jiggle, putting on a show.
Raccoons wear hats made of dirt,
As garden gnomes chuckle, in their shirts.

Onions cry, but they don't weep,
Hiding beneath, where secrets sleep.
Rabbits gossip 'bout the radishes,
While carrots dream of daring wishes.

Digging deep, there's laughter found,
As trowels tango on the ground.
What treasures lie beneath the moss?
Even mushrooms have a gossip gloss!

So if you peek near the old oak tree,
Listen closely, you'll hear the glee.
The soil whispers tales of delight,
Of leafy jokes and playful nights.

Petals on the Path

A daisy waved at a passing bee,
"Don't you stop? Come chat with me!"
But the bee buzzed off, saying, "Not today,
I'm on a diet, can't you say?"

Tulips strut, all dressed in style,
They wink at passersby with a smile.
"Oh look, it's us, the floral trend,
Let's dazzle the dandelions, my friend!"

Roses giggle, thinking they're grand,
Their fragrant charms are completely planned.
But lilies shout, "Oh, please refrain,
It's not a race, we'll just entertain!"

As petals flutter, what do they know?
They dance and prance in a colorful show.
Every step on this flowery lane,
Brings laughter, sunshine, and joy unstained.

Sunlit Petals

Under the sun, they spin and sway,
Laughing petals in a bright ballet.
But watch out, they may steal your hat,
And wear it proudly, just like that!

Buttercups giggle, asking for sun,
As violets munch on cookies for fun.
"Did you hear the tulips' silly joke?
About the leafy lad, who went up in smoke?"

Dandelions puff with a snicker or two,
"Catch us if you can, we'll float to the blue!"
As bees join in with their jangly tune,
They dance on the petals, like a silly cartoon.

Sunsets blush with colors so bright,
While petals chuckle at the drifting light.
So join the fun, don't be afraid,
In the warmth of the sun, let joy cascade!

The Language of Flowers

Roses speak in whispers, sweet and bold,
They tell of secrets, quietly told.
But daisies shout, "We're all just friends!"
In the garden where laughter never ends.

Ivy creeps in, with tales of old,
And violets giggle, their stories unfold.
"Did you hear what the sunflowers said?
'We're the tallest, but sleep in bed!'"

Lilies ponder, with a thoughtful gaze,
While pansies strike silly poses for praise.
"Watch out for the bees on a sugar spree,
Floral humor's as sweet as can be!"

So gather your blooms, let the giggles start,
In the garden of glee, we'll share our heart.
For every flower speaks in its way,
Creating laughter throughout the day.

A Palette of Memories

A flower tried to tell a joke,
But ended up just making smoke.
With colors bright, it lost its flair,
As bees buzzed by without a care.

A daisy danced with all its might,
While tulips frowned at its delight.
It's rare to see a bloom so bold,
The story of a flower told!

A sunflower wore a silly hat,
While violets chit-chatted with a cat.
Their laughter echoed through the day,
In this bright garden, come what may.

So grab a brush, and paint a scene,
With flowers giggling, bright, and clean.
Memories bloom in colors wild,
Each laugh a petal, light and mild.

Echoed in the Garden

In a patch of green, a rose once sang,
With a voice as sweet as a little fang.
It hit a note, the bees went mad,
A flower chorus — oh, how they rapped!

A tulip chimed in, off-key and loud,
While daisies formed a wobbly crowd.
They swayed and buzzed, hilarious sight,
In the garden, from day to night.

"Oh dear, oh dear!" said a marigold,
"I think I've sprouted a little mold!"
But laughter rang as the flowers swayed,
With humor shining, they never frayed.

So sing along, let your petals sway,
In this garden where giggles play.
Echoes of joy in the sunlit air,
As flowers laugh without a care.

Seeds of Hope

A tiny seed once dreamed out loud,
Of world travels, big and proud.
It hopped on soil, with glee it spun,
In a race with worms, oh, what fun!

It met a beetle with jokes to share,
Together they danced, without a care.
A ladybug joined, cracking a grin,
In this playful realm where all can win.

They whispered tales of rain and sun,
Of how to sprout and just be fun.
With every jig, the earth gave cheer,
Seeds of hope grow, year after year.

So plant a dream, just wait and see,
What wonders bloom with humor and glee.
In gardens bright, where laughter flows,
Let your imagination sprout and grow!

The Circle of Seasons

Spring brought laughter and jokes galore,
With flowers pranking — oh, what a score!
While summer teased with brilliant rays,
Making blooms dance through sun-kissed days.

Autumn giggled, casting colorful leaves,
As flowers whispered, "What a crazy breeze!"
Winter chuckled in frosty white,
Covering blooms, yet still feeling bright.

A squirrel took charge, acting quite spry,
Dressed in blooms, oh my, oh my!
He juggled acorns, a comic to see,
Nature's laughter, wild and free.

So let the seasons spin around,
In gardens where funny dreams abound.
Through every bloom, let laughter rise,
In the circle of seasons, where joy lies!

Sunlit Blossom Tales

In the garden, flowers prance,
Dancing gaily, what a chance!
Petunias giggle, daisies cheer,
Every bloom holds laughter near.

Buttercups wear sunny grins,
While violets drum on pots like twins.
Tulips tell jokes to bees in flight,
With every buzz, the day feels bright.

Snapdragons snap at passing shoes,
They're the clowns in nature's news.
As bees mistake them for a snack,
A humorous garden, never lacks!

When pansies wink, who can resist?
They throw a party! Don't insist.
Join the fun, it's flower time,
Nature's jesters in bloom, oh-so-prime!

The Essence of Fragility

A dainty bloom with frilled attire,
Sways in the breeze, a comedy choir.
A breeze goes by, and oh, what fun!
They tumble over, so light, they run.

With every gust, they seem to play,
Who will stand tall by end of day?
Dandelions sing, 'we're tougher yet!'
Fragile? Please! We're no cornet!

In sunlight, they burst into fits,
Fluffy seeds flying like tiny wits.
'Catch me if you can!' they cheerfully shout,
Floating away with a playful pout.

Come rain or shine, they break the mold,
These fragile flowers are brave and bold.
With a wink and a giggle, they know their game,
In life's fragility, they stake their claim!

Resilient in Bloom

From cracks in concrete, they emerge,
Little fighters, making a surge.
With petals bright, they're here to stay,
Cracking jokes in their flowery way.

Through storms they bow, but never break,
With laughter loud, their stance they take.
Who knew weeds could hold such mirth?
Resilience blooms, bringing forth worth.

They wear their scars like stars on night,
Cracks on their stems show strength in light.
'We've got this!' they giggle aloud,
Nature's quirkiest flower crowd!

In gardens wild, where laughter thrives,
Resilient blooms lead happy lives.
From the dirt, they rise with grace,
In their funny dance, find a place!

Petals of Perseverance

Small flowers grow in the toughest spots,
Cracks in sidewalks? They'll take the shots.
With a chuckle, they shoot for the sky,
'We'll show the world how to really fly!'

Each petal tells tales of battles won,
In every bloom, there's warmth from the sun.
Struggling hard? They simply laugh,
Making a joke out of a tough path.

No fancy gardens, just dirt and grit,
But look at them dance, they never quit.
Chasing the rainbows with joyful leaps,
In petals of hope, their spirit keeps.

So here's to flowers, resilient and bold,
With humor in blooms, their stories unfold.
In every crack, a brave heart beats,
Perseverance shines—what a feat!

The Dance of the Tulips

Tulips in a line, they sway and they twirl,
Their floppy little heads give giggles a whirl.
They seem to be teasing the bees in their flight,
With colors so bright, oh what a silly sight!

A wind swoops in, they stumble and fall,
Like dancers who've tripped at the grandest ball.
They bounce back quickly, with a cheeky grin,
As if they'd rehearsed their wild little spin!

The garden is laughing, it's quite the affair,
As tulips keep jiving without a care.
They whisper, they chuckle, in terpsichore's bliss,
Who knew that a flower could do such a twist?

So when you walk by, give a cheer and a clap,
For tulips who dance with each sunny suntrap.
In this floral cabaret, you'll find such delight,
With floppy tulips bringing laughter so bright!

Under the Arbor's Shade

Under the arbor, where flowers convene,
Petunias are plotting a garden routine.
With whispers and giggles, they scheme and they plot,
To pull off a joke that's quite bold, it's a lot!

Daisies and roses, they join in the fun,
While sunflowers grin, soaking up the bright sun.
They decide to prank, as the squirrels scurry by,
By tying their stems with some twine to the sky!

When breezes come dancing, the flowers all sway,
Their strings overhead in a tangled ballet.
The squirrels are flustered, they scamper and dash,
While flowers just giggle, this prank's quite the smash!

So if you stroll through, look up to the trees,
And laugh at the flowers, just swaying with ease.
Under the shade where they conspire and play,
The garden is bursting with laughter today!

Symphony of the Garden

Bees buzzing basslines while daisies hum high,
Tulips tap-tap dance as the wind passes by.
A symphony blooms, with notes made of cheer,
In this leafy concert, there's nothing to fear!

The lilies hit cymbals, with petals so grand,
While violets giggle in a synchronized band.
Each flower's a singer, each leaf is a thrill,
A rollicking rhythm that gives a good chill!

The snails form a chorus, with slugs in the back,
As worms add the harmony, keeping the track.
Everyone's playing, not missing a beat,
This garden's a stage, and it simply can't be beat!

So dance and so sing, join nature's fine tune,
With flowers who giggle beneath the bright moon.
This symphony blooms, let the good times unfold,
In a world where the garden's the grandest of gold!

Flourish and Fade

In a garden so jolly, where wonders abound,
Some flowers grow tall, while others stay round.
The daisies are struttin', so proud of their place,
While petunias insist they can win in the race!

"I'm taller!" shouts one, "I bloom all day long!"
While marigolds chuckle, "Oh, you're very wrong!"
With colors ablaze and pinks that gleam bright,
This garden's a riot, such whimsical sight!

But soon comes a breeze, as the sun starts to wane,
And flowers all whisper about fortune and fame.
"Let's flourish," they cheer, "and then fade with a blast,
We'll be legends in petals, a shadowy cast!"

So dance while you can, enjoy blooms while they last,
For time is a trickster, it travels so fast.
Yet laughter remains, as flowers exit stage,
With memories blooming, let's turn the next page!

A Bloom in the Night

In the garden, quite absurd,
A flower danced, it was unheard.
It swayed to the moon's bright tune,
Singing loudly like a loony boon.

The bees all laughed, they couldn't keep straight,
As petals jived, it was quite the fate.
A sunflower tried to join the fun,
But tripped on roots—oh, what a run!

The nightingales joined in with cheer,
Chomping snacks, the blooms had no fear.
With twinkling lights and giggles so tight,
The garden turned wild, a true delight!

By dawn, they slumbered, each petal tucked,
With dreams of antics, they were all plucked.
No seeds left for planting, silly and bright,
A blooming party that lasted all night!

Rooted in Love

There once was a tree with secrets to share,
With roots so tangled, it had flair.
It whispered sweet nothings to daisies near,
And left them giggling, bright-eyed with cheer.

A rose snickered, 'You can't woo me, dude!'
While tulips chuckled, 'You're making a shrewd.'
Yet day after day, they'd all gather 'round,
Listening to love in the roots underground.

The wind joined in, a mischievous gale,
Twirling the leaves like a floral tale.
They'd sing to the stars, each note full of glee,
As branches would sway, drinks spilled on the spree!

So next time you stroll past that old tree,
Remember the laughter—it's not just for free.
With roots in the ground and joy up above,
Nature's a stage for the stories of love!

The Secrets We Hold

In a garden so lush, a grapevine would brag,
About juicy gossip, it liked to snag.
The daisies would giggle, 'Oh, do spill the tea!'
While thorns rolled their eyes, 'Just let it be!'

A daffodil winked, 'I've seen more than you!'
'Like what?' asked the tulips, all brightly in hue.
'Well, that one time, that beetle, you know,
Thought he'd impress with his bumpy cool show!'

The sunflowers laughed like a chorus on sky,
'Their dance moves were awful, oh my, oh my!'
'But what about you, with your head held so high?
You're not a dancer, just a seed up to fly!'

So secrets entwined in a floral parade,
As leaves shared antics, connections were made.
In the world under blossoms, a jolly old game,
With giggles and whispers, they all claimed their fame!

Nature's Embrace

In the arms of the forest, a squirrel stood tall,
With acorns and nuts, he'd grandly enthrall.
He'd throw a small party with branches and leaves,
While critters would come in their party weaves.

A hedgehog pranced in a fancy bow tie,
While rabbits hopped high, saying, 'Oh my, oh my.'
The owls hooted loudly, a DJ on cue,
With forest tunes playing, it was quite the zoo!

The flowers were twirling, all colors and spice,
With roses in sequins and violets in vice.
They laughed and they danced till the moon took her place,
In the high of the night, all in nature's embrace.

As dawn started peeking, the party was done,
With smiles on their faces, each creature had fun.
In the heart of the woods, relationships bloom,
As laughter and joy fill the forest with room!

The Artistry of Nature

In gardens where daisies feel grand,
A sunflower sways, takes a stand.
Bees buzzing loud in their parade,
While roses giggle, unafraid.

Butterflies dance, a colorful crew,
Winking at thorns, 'We're lovely too!'
The lilies chuckle, in their own way,
While the wind joins in, starts to play.

The ants march up like tiny tanks,
While grasshoppers leap with their pranks.
In this whimsy, nature's delight,
Where laughter blooms, oh what a sight!

So tip your hat to the blooms and the bees,
Join the chorus of rustling leaves.
For in each garden, humor's bright hue,
Nature's canvas, a riot of view!

The Seasons' Chorus

Winter whispers with blankets of white,
While squirrels decide to take flight.
Spring follows in with a giggling breeze,
Tickling the trees, bringing them to tease.

Summer bursts in, oh what a show,
Ice cream cones and sweat from the flow.
Autumn dances, in colors so bold,
Turning trees into stories to be told.

As seasons twist in their silly ways,
They share their quirks in playful displays.
Nature's joke, round and around,
In this funny dance, joy is found.

So laugh with the leaves as they spin,
Join the seasons, let the fun begin!
In every cycle, a chuckle resides,
Through every change, the laughter abides!

Echoing Sweetness

A donut-shaped flower, so round and sweet,
Giggling at bees, 'Can you handle this treat?'
Nectar's the laughter, it's honey they bring,
Nature's chorus in buzzing, they sing.

Raspberry bushes whisper secrets they keep,
While birds around chatter, chirp, and peep.
The wind runs wild, teasing the blooms,
Tickling their petals, overjoyed in rooms.

Violets boast of their deep purple hue,
'We're the trendsetters of pretty,' they coo.
Dandelions puff out their fluffy white hair,
Leaving wishes dancing softly in air.

So savor the sweetness that nature supplies,
And laugh with each bloom as humor defies.
In echoes of joy, let the giggles resound,
For in every flower, pure fun can be found!

And Yet They Rise

In cracks of the pavement, some daisies pop,
Saying, 'Excuse us, we won't stop!'
Though life is tough and the weather might frown,
They bloom with a grin, never backing down.

Sunflowers stretch to heights they adore,
'Look at me, I'm a tower, give me more!'
While pansies pout, with their colorful frowns,
Creating confetti in the bustling towns.

The little sprouts joke with the tallest trees,
'Growing tall? We got this, just watch us ease.'
Against all odds, with a spark and a wit,
They rise with a laugh, refusing to quit.

So dance in the garden, don't run or hide,
For every flower is a joyride.
In life's funny garden, with laughter we thrive,
And yet through the struggle, we humorously rise!

Echoes of Vibrant Grace

In the garden, bees do dance,
Wearing tiny polka dots by chance.
Roses giggle, lilies sway,
Sunflowers splash, come what may.

Butterflies in frilly hats,
Planning teas with clever chats.
Daisies wear a crown of glee,
As buzzing friends join in with tea.

A Tapestry of Color

Painted petals, bright and bold,
Mimic stories yet untold.
Tulips in a silly line,
Laugh at weeds that try to shine.

Violets wear their shades of blue,
Huddled close like a lively crew.
Breezes toss their jobs around,
As blooms gather for a sound.

Blossoms in the Breeze

Dandelions with a wishful grin,
Play hide and seek where dreams begin.
Crickets joke in leafy towers,
Making plans to steal some flowers.

Orchids drop their elegant pretenses,
Giggling at the grass's expenses.
With every gust, they spin and twirl,
Sprinkling joy upon the world.

Nature's Whispered Elegy

Petunias whisper tales of light,
As shadows gather, soft and slight.
Jasmine chuckles, sweet perfume,
While daisies plot to burst the gloom.

Cacti wear their prickly shoes,
Launching jests that bloom with hues.
In every rustle, laughter flows,
As nature winks and gently glows.

In Bloom's Embrace

In the garden, flowers play,
Dancing petals every day.
Bees wear tiny dancing shoes,
Buzzing tunes in vibrant hues.

Sunflowers wink, it's quite absurd,
Who knew they'd play the rumor bird?
Roses gossip with gentle sighs,
While tulips roll their playful eyes.

Daisies laugh at silly bees,
Tickling winds through fragrant leaves.
Each bloom sings a quirky song,
In a world where all belongs.

Laughter spreads with fragrant cheer,
In this plot, no room for fear.
Let's twirl in colorful delight,
In bloom's embrace, we dance all night!

A Garden's Soliloquy

In the garden, a sunflower stands,
Speaking strongly with leafy hands.
'Why can't daisies keep still?' it muses,
'Always wiggling, what are their uses?'

A rose replies with crimson flair,
'They're dreaming of a fresh spring air!'
Lilies laugh, a giggling band,
Sharing whispers close at hand.

The violets join in with snickers,
As ants march by in little flickers.
'If only we could stretch our arms,
And shoo away those pesky charms!'

Yet every bloom, from bud to leaf,
Holds secrets spun in joy and grief.
In this garden, tales unfold,
With giggles wrapped in colors bold.

Mournful Petals

Once a flower, bright and proud,
Now it shrinks beneath a cloud.
'Oh dear me, my colors fade,'
Sighs the bloom in shadow laid.

The wind whispers with gentle cheer,
'There's no need for mournful fear!'
But the petals droop, they pout,
'What's this fuss all about?'

A beetle chuckles, rolling by,
'You've got to laugh, or you'll just cry!'
Petals tremble, then they giggle,
Finding joy in every wiggle.

So they dance with every sway,
Not a droop left in their way.
Mournful petals, now set free,
Laughing wild as they just be!

The Light of Petal Paths

Along the paths where blossoms gleam,
There lies a light, a fragrant dream.
Petals prance in the morning glow,
In a joyful, colorful flow.

Butterflies flutter in crazy loops,
Toppling daisies, drawing scoops.
The tulips giggle, trying to chase,
All the giggling at the race.

Shimmering lights, oh how they tease,
While the daisies sway in the breeze.
'Come, join our fun, don't be shy!'
The flowers call to passersby.

With skipping steps and hearts so light,
They dance, they laugh, in pure delight.
The petal paths invite us all,
To join the bloom in nature's ball!

A Garden of Resilience

In a garden so bright, flowers stand tall,
They juggle the rain, they have a ball.
With a wiggle and giggle, they dance in the breeze,
Who knew tough little buds could be so at ease?

Among tangled weeds, they wear a crown,
Swaying and laughing, never a frown.
Silly little daisies, in ridiculous hats,
Show us their style, those quirky little spats.

When storms try to battle, they just stamp their roots,
Giving the thunder a pair of old boots.
With a chuckle they grow through each drizzle and storm,

In their plush little kingdom, they're never forlorn.

In this garden of giggles, the lessons are clear,
With humor and joy, there's nothing to fear.
So let's plant a few jokes deep into the ground,
And watch as our laughter blooms all around!

The Blooming Heart

A heart made of blossoms, so vibrant and wild,
With petals like laughter from each playful child.
It whispers sweet secrets from dusk until dawn,
As it twirls and it twinkles on each lovely lawn.

In the meadow of mischief, the blooms start to tease,
They play leapfrog with sunshine and tickle the breeze.
With a wink and a nod, they twirl round and round,
Who knew flowers could disco to such vibrant sound?

Through pruning and planting, they're cheeky and spry,
Spreading their fragrance as bees buzz by.
With jokes in their seams and giggles to share,
These blooms of the heart know beyond all compare.

On Valentine's Day, they throw quite a bash,
With petals like confetti, they make such a splash.
So here's to the blooms that dance in delight,
With laughter and joy, they make life so bright!

Dance of the Wildflowers

Wildflowers prance in a colorful spree,
Doing the cha-cha, so wild and so free.
With each little petal, they flutter about,
Turning serious gardens into a grand bout.

They flirt with the wind, in skirts made of gold,
Showing off colors that never get old.
In a party of pollen, they giggle and sway,
Who said wildflowers couldn't dance every day?

They twirl with the daisies, they play with the bees,
Spreading their joy on the shimmering breeze.
With twinkling bright laughter, they gather in crews,
Creating a festival, filled with all hues.

From the tallest of stems to the tiniest buds,
They laugh in the sunlight, surrounded by floods.
So let's join the dance, have our fun and play,
With wildflowers leading, let's kick the blues away!

Horizon of Blossoms

On the horizon of blossoms, where colors collide,
The flowers are squabbling, but it's all done with pride.
With giggles and jibes, they embrace the day,
Each bloom has a tale, in its own funny way.

They argue about sunshine, who gets the most light,
As the violets tease the tulips in flight.
With a snicker or two, they poke fun at the trees,
"Your bark may be tough, but we'll dance in the breeze!"

They bloom all together, in a riotous cheer,
The wind is their partner, no worries or fear.
With smiles on their faces, they wink at the skies,
Creating a panorama that delights every eye.

So here's to the blossoms, let's give them a clap,
Their humor and joy fill the world like a map.
Across every horizon, let laughter ignite,
In the garden of giggles, the future is bright!

The Heart of the Orchid

In a garden, an orchid pranced,
Swaying dreams, it cheerily danced.
With petals that giggled with glee,
Whispering secrets, wild and free.

A bee came buzzing, eyes aglow,
Said, "Your elegance steals the show!"
The orchid grinned, said, "Please be kind,
But I'm the star—don't you mind!"

They shared a laugh, what a scene!
In the bloom of laughter, life's so keen.
A garden most joyous, and so bright,
In silliness blooming, day or night.

So if you see a flower tease,
Know it's humor, aiming to please.
With a twist of bloom, and a wink of cheer,
The heart of the orchid draws us near.

Petals as Promises

Petals tossed like silly notes,
Whispers of wishes on playful floats.
Each color a chuckle, each scent a grin,
In the garden of giggles, where fun begins.

A daisy declared, "I'm the queen!"
While the roses laughed in shades of green.
"You think you're great? Just wait and see!"
As petals swirled in a joyful spree.

Tulips tripped in their fancy gowns,
Fell over petals, making amusing sounds.
In a bouquet of laughter, they surely unite,
All promises blossom in pure delight.

So join the blooms in their silly scheme,
Laughing along, as they weave a dream.
With petals as promises, bright and loud,
In this floral jest, let's all be proud!

The Secret Life of Flowers

Under the sun, flowers conspire,
Telling tales that spark desire.
A tulip said with a cheeky grin,
"I've hidden a snicker beneath my skin!"

Roses whisper of love, oh so grand,
But dandelions have a cheeky plan.
They blow their seeds with all their might,
Saying, "Catch us if you think you're bright!"

Sunflowers stretch, tall and proud,
Waving hello, to every crowd.
But when the breeze does start to tease,
They bend and sway with charming ease.

In this secret life, oh what fun,
Every flower shines under the sun.
With laughter and joy, their stories unfurl,
A whimsically vibrant, secret world.

Blossoms in the Storm

In a storm, the blossoms sway,
Shouting, "Look at us, we're here to play!"
Though winds may howl and dark clouds loom,
They shimmy and shake, dispelling gloom.

A brave little bud shouted out loud,
"Rain's just a shower—a riotous crowd!"
With lightning cracking, they danced in delight,
Wiping away worries, shining so bright.

Petals soaked, they laughed at the downpour,
In the heart of chaos, they wanted more.
Each droplet a tickle, a fun little game,
And the flowers, they whispered with joy, not shame.

So if storms come with thunderous roars,
Remember the blossoms, as fun as outdoors.
For in every tempest, they find their way,
In laughter and joy, they bloom and play.